Bennett Cerf's

Book of

ANIMAL

illustrated by *Roy McKie*

This title was originally catalogued by the Library of Congress as follows: Cerf, Bennett Alfred. Book of animal riddles. Illustrated by Roy McKie. New York, Beginner Books, 1964. 62 p. col. illus. 24 cm. "B-34." 1. Riddles. I. Title. PN6371.C348 j793.7   64—11246   ISBN 0-394-80034-6   ISBN 0-394-90034-0 (lib. bdg.)

RIDDLES

BEGINNER BOOKS

A Division of Random House, Inc.

IJ   5 6 7 8

How do you stop
a dog from barking
in the back seat of a car?

Have him sit in front with you.

What animals need to be oiled?

Mice do.
They squeak.

6

What kind of bird is like a car?

A goose is like a car.

They both go honk.

When is it bad luck
to have a black cat
follow you?

When you are a mouse.

What is a good way
to keep a dog
off the street?

Put him in a barking lot.

Why are fish so smart?

They always go around
in schools.

Why is it hard to talk
with a goat around?

Because he always
butts in.

What hurts more than
a giraffe with a sore throat?

17

A centipede with sore feet.

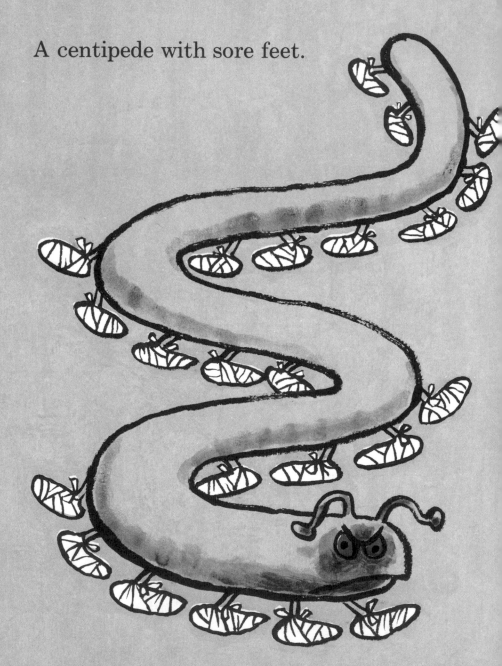

What is gray,

   has big ears,

     a long trunk,

      and weighs only three pounds?

A very, very, very thin elephant.

Ten cats were in a boat.

One jumped out.

How many were left?

None were left.

All the rest were copycats.

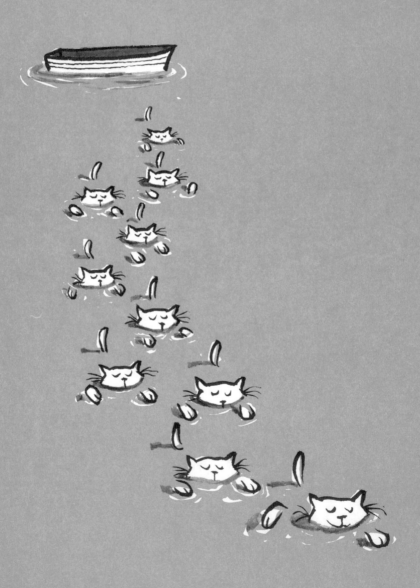

Name six things
smaller than
the mouth of an ant.

Six of his teeth.

What kind of pine

has the sharpest needles?

A porcupine.

Put three ducks
in a box.
What do you have?

A box of quackers.

What is it?

It has four legs.

It eats hay.

It has a tail.

And it sees just as well

from either end.

A horse with his eyes shut.

What animal can carry
the most on his back?

The snail.

He carries his house on his back.

If your dog ate your book,
what would you do?

I would take the words
right out of his mouth.

What has two heads,

one tail,

four legs on one side,

and two legs on the other?

A horse

with a lady

riding sideways.

Would you rather have
an elephant chase you or
a lion?

I would rather have
the elephant chase the lion.

HUMMMMMMM

HUMM

HUMMMMm

HUMMm

HUMMM

HUMMMM

Why does a humming bird hum?

Because he doesn't know the words.

How did the turtle
keep three jumps
ahead of the rabbit?

He played checkers with the rabbit.

When is it all right

to drink milk from a saucer?

When you are a cat.

What must a stork do
to stand on one foot?

Hold up the other one.

When do you put a frog
in your sister's bed?

When you can't catch a mouse.

What must you know
before you teach a dog tricks?

More than the dog.

When did the fly fly?

When the spider spied her.

Why don't you put
an ad in the paper
when you've lost your dog?

Dogs can't read.

Which side of a hen
has the most feathers?

The outside.

What is better

than a dog that can count?

A spelling bee.

What is it?

It has a hump.

It is brown.

It can go all day without drinking water.

And it sings like a canary.

I give up.

A camel.

But a camel
doesn't sing
like a canary.

61

I know it.
I just put that in
to make it harder.